What a wonderful
thing string is!
Just think of the things
you can do with string!

For John and Anna with love
J.H.

For Anne Veronica, with love
M.C.

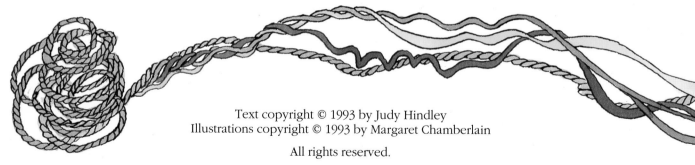

Text copyright © 1993 by Judy Hindley
Illustrations copyright © 1993 by Margaret Chamberlain

First U.S. edition 1993
Published in Great Britain in 1993 by Walker Books Ltd., London.

Library of Congress Cataloging-in-Publication Data:

Hindley, Judy.
A piece of string is a wonderful thing / Judy Hindley :
illustrated by Margaret Chamberlain.—1st U.S. ed.
Summary: Relates in verse the origin and uses of string.
1. String—Juvenile literature. [1. String.]
I. Chamberlain, Margaret, ill. II. Title. III. Series
TS1785.H56 1993   677'.71—dc20   92-53137
ISBN 1-56402-147-5

10 9 8 7 6 5 4 3 2 1

Printed in Hong Kong

The illustrations in this book were done in inks,
watercolor, gouache, and acrylic paints.

Candlewick Press
2067 Massachusetts Avenue
Cambridge, Massachusetts 02140

A PIECE of STRING

IS A WONDERFUL THING

Judy Hindley

illustrated by Margaret Chamberlain

CANDLEWICK PRESS

CAMBRIDGE, MASSACHUSETTS

Let us sing a song
about string—
what a wonderful thing it is!
When you think of the things
that you do with string,
you have to admit
it's a marvelous bit
to have in your kit:

My friend's uncle said, "You should never go anywhere without change for a phone call, a pencil stub, and a piece of string."

for a fishing line, a boat, a kite,
somewhere to hang your socks to dry;
for tying up packages, fastening gates,
leading you safe through a treacherous cave;
for a spinning top, a skipping rope,
a bracelet, a necklace, a drawstring purse . . .
there's just about no end of things
a person can do with a piece of string!
And then you wonder,
from time to time,
how did a thing like
string begin?

← slipknot

A slipknot can hitch
a boat, a horse,
a swing...

three small knots   three big knots   three small knots

= ... --- ...
= Morse code for S.O.S.

Back in the days
when mammoths roamed,
and they didn't have chains
and they didn't have ropes
for hauling around or
lifting things up—

The bodies of birds and animals are worked by living strings called sinews.

(well, they didn't have any connecting things:
buttons or braces or buckles or laces,
or latches or catches or bolts or belts,
or tabs or clasps or hooks and eyes . . .
Velcro patches! ribbons! ties!
zips or grips or snaps or clips)—
well how did anyone
THINK IT UP?

About 2.5 million years ago, people were chipping stones to make a cutting edge, but it took us 2 million years to get the edge sharp enough to cut out leather strips.

In New Guinea, people make fishing nets out of spiderwebs. They leave a wooden frame with a colony of spiders, who spin their webs around it. In the British Museum, I saw a spiderweb hat that was made this way.

Did they chat as they sat
near the fire at night,
eating their prehistoric fish,
and say, "What we need
to get it right
is a thing like hair,
but long and strong,
a thing to tie on a piece of bone:
what a wonderful fishing line
that would make!"?

After which, I suppose,
they went out to the lake
and tickled the fish
with their cold, bare hands—
for they didn't have nets
if they didn't have string.
How they all must have wished
that they had such a thing!

For a long time the only spears were pointed sticks.
Much later, a chip of stone would be tied to
the stick with a sinew.

So how on earth
do you think they discovered it?
Do you think somebody
just tripped over it?
Was it an accident?
Was it a guess?
Did it emerge
from a hideous mess?
Did it begin with
a sinuous twig,
a whippety willow,
a snaky vine?

In order to hunt successfully, people had to start working as a team.
But there's always a slowpoke...

Did it happen that somebody, one dark night,
winding his weary way home alone,
got tripped by the foot on a loop of vine
and fell kersplat! and broke a bone;
and then, as he lay in the dark, so sad,
and yelled for help (and it didn't come)
he got thoroughly bored with doing that
and invented—a woolly-rhinoceros trap?

Teams of hunters drove their prey over cliffs
or possibly into holes hidden by vines.

Oh, it might have occurred in a number of ways
as the populace pondered the fate they faced—
as they huddled in caves
in the worst of the weather,
wishing for things like
tents
and clothes,
as they hugged furry skins
to their shivering bodies
and scraps of hide
to their cold, bare toes

In time, ancient hunters learned to use sinews to string their bows.

"If only there was something to join our clothes together ..."

And they had no suspenders
or snaps or connectors
or buttons or toggles
or zippers or pins—
so HOW did they hold up their trousers, then?
They must have said,
"Oh! A piece of string
would be SUCH a fine thing
to have around the cave!"

The very first needles were probably thorns.

One hunting breakthrough was the bolas — three stones tied to a leather strap or a sinew. It was thrown around an animal's legs to trip it.

Things on strings are a glamorous way to deck your body.
Think of necklaces, pendants, belts, and bracelets.

They needed a noose for an antelope foot.
They needed a thing to string a bow.
They needed nets, and traps, and snares
for catching their venison unaware
and leading the first wild horses home.

Well, they must've gone on to try and try
as hundreds of thousands of years went by,
twisting and braiding and trying out knots
with strips of hide and rhinoceros guts,
spiders' webs and liana vines,
reeds and weeds and ribs of palm,
slippery sinews, muscles, and thongs,
elephant grasses three feet long,
and wriggly fish-bone skeletons.

fish trap

antler harpoon ~ a spear with a string attached

antler spearhead

And they spun out the fibers
of vegetable fluff,
and they felted the hairs of a goat,
and they knitted and twisted
and braided and twined

A single fiber of wool is as strong as a thread of gold.

SPINNING A THIN THING FROM A FAT THING
Yarn is spun from sheep's fleece, cotton tufts, or even birds' down.
Try spinning with cotton. Pull and stretch it very gently,
very steadily, twisting it really tight as it draws out.

and invented . . .

TURNING A THIN THING INTO A FLAT THING

The next trick is weaving and knitting to make fabric.
Tiny short hairs laid down higgledy-piggledy, then
wetted and pressed together, can be turned into felt.

the three-ply rope!
What a wonderful thing!
A very fine thing!
The KING of string
is rope!

Making Rope

One man twists two strands clockwise and walks forward.

A second man makes sure the strands of rope are laid tightly together.

A third man closes the strands by twisting this tool counterclockwise and walks backward as the rope is formed.

The Egyptians made rope from bulrushes, camel hair, and flax.

The oldest rope ever discovered came from a tomb in Egypt. It was made from flax 5000 years ago.

Sometimes rope was even made from women's hair.

You can lift up pots
from an echoing well with it,
fling it to make a bridge;
you can haul along hulking hunks
of stone for building a pyramid
(and they did).

measuring a field

using a plumb line

making sure stone is flat

bringing water from the well

You can also halter and harness
your animal friends.

The first plow was probably just
a forked branch tied to an ox.

Our earliest picture of a sailing boat
is on a 3000-year-old Egyptian pot.

And then again, when life gets tough
and it's time to be moving along,
you can use it to lash your luggage fast
to a camel, a goat, a raft, a boat—
oh! a stringable thing
is the only thing
to have when you're afloat!

But they still
went on and on,
sticking and spinning
and looping and gluing
and tying and trying out
more and more types,
quicker and quicker
crazier, slicker

early cart

The pontoon bridge was an early bright idea. It began with a row of boats all roped together.

Roman crane

early gravity railway

Isambard Kingdom Brunel went up in a hot-air balloon to lay the first rope of the famous Clifton Suspension Bridge in Bristol, England.

early flying machine

Hot metal can be stretched into rails and cables, ropes, and delicate wires.

for pulleys and ladders
and hoses and bridges
and fences and winches
and wires and pipes.

Where on earth
have we come to now?
What would a town
ever do without string
and things that go stringing along?
Candlewicks, rackets, and violins,
telephones, plumbing, and railroad lines,
things that fasten and fuse and fix
and click and stick and link.

Can you even begin
to count the ways
that things connect
with other things?
It could just about
scramble your brain!

And to think it began
(though we'll never know when)
with somebody choking
on elephant gristle,
or trying to chew
through the stem
of a thistle,
or just stumbling into
the thing!

Oh, what we've done
with a piece of string
is a marvelous thing,
an amazing thing—
some would say
a crazy thing!
And one of these days
I might just go away
and begin it
all over
again . . .

Can you even begin
to count the things you
can do with string?
It could just about
scramble your brain!
When reading this book,
don't forget to look at both
kinds of words:
this kind
and *this kind*.